Advance praise for STUTTERS

Mary Ricketson's new book of poems—*Stutters*—is accurate as a chickadee's chirp or an arrow's sting. The poet creates a legacy varied as the soil's grains scattering from opening fingers.

—Shelby Stephenson was poet laureate of North Carolina from 2015-2018. His recent books are *Country, Praises* and *Cow Mire Songs.*

Mary Ricketson invokes the inner courage of a personal difference seeking to come to light. Her poetry warms our hearts with its raw passion and fear, its joys and sorrows. As told over the course of her lifetime, she shares her stories within the voice of a stutterer, bringing us into her realm. Mary shines a light on what it's like to want to speak but often having to change her pattern or her words or even avoiding speaking at all, for fear of what might or might not emerge from her lips and throat. Mary's humility shines through in this book of poetry, as does her bravery, charm, and wit.

As a speech language pathologist with over 26 years of clinical practice, I can attest to Mary Ricketson's hard-earned fluency today. As a colleague working with Mary with a local non-profit, I can attest to her dedication to women and to voices often not heard. Hearing Mary speak and recite her poetry is a time-stand-still kind of experience. Her canter draws you in, and though there is an occasional stutter or repetition, she has a bravery that elevates her through the moment and onto further words and prose. This is a most unique book of poetry. When I read her words on these pages, I feel she is here speaking them aloud to me in her own beautiful, passionate, and fluent, as well as disfluent, way.

—Emory E Prescott, PhD, MS,CCC-SLP, author of *The Herbal Brain*

Mary Ricketson's book, *Stutters, A Book of Hope*, takes the reader through Ricketson's journey of fear and frustration. Every word is a struggle. In school, "Children tease, mock, mimic...copy my dreaded stutter." Ricketson suffers shame "tension grows like weeds." This book pulls at your heart's strings. It's honest and fascinating. Her voice finally responds to practicing rhythm and she finds peace in the healing power of nature. Ricketson's courage and strength shine through the pages. This book is informative and an amazing story of a woman who overcomes the storms of life. Ricketson writes with candor about her son who also stutters. Families struggling in the shadows of stuttering will find hope in this collection of poems.

—Brenda Kay Ledford, MA; Retired Educator; Author of: *Blanche, Poems of a Blue Ridge Woman* and *Leatherwood Falls, Blue Ridge Mountain Poems*

In Mary Ricketson's latest poetry book she shares with us a look at her personal life. At the age of seven Mary began stuttering as she tried to speak. She allows us to see the pain and embarrassment it caused her. Yet, despite this obstacle, she was determined to push past it and achieve her goals. Mary completed college, became a counselor and a poet. She has excelled in both places, thus helping and inspiring many people. This is a special read.

—Glenda Barrett, author of *When the Sap Rises*, and *The Beauty of Silence*.

Stutters

A Book of Hope

Poems

Mary Ricketson

Copyright © 2023 Mary Ricketson

All rights reserved. No part of this publication may be reproduced, distributed, or transmitted in any form or by any means, including photocopying, recording, or other electronic or mechanical methods, without the prior written permission of the publisher, except in the case of brief quotations embodied in critical reviews and certain other noncommercial uses permitted by copyright law. For permission requests, write to the publisher, addressed "Attention: Permissions Coordinator," at the address below.

Redhawk Publications
The Catawba Valley Community College Press
2550 Hwy 70 SE
Hickory, NC 28602

Ordering Information:
Quantity sales. Special discounts are available on quantity purchases by corporations, associations, and others. For details, contact the publisher at the address above.

ISBN: 978-1-959346-20-3

Library of Congress Control Number: 20233944572

Printed in the United States of America

Dedicated to my son, Lee

Poetry Previously Published by Mary Ricketson

Disorgananza, private collection 2000

I Hear the River Call my Name, Finishing Line Press 2007

Hanging Dog Creek, Future Cycle Press, 2014

Shade and Shelter, Kelsay Books 2018

Mississippi: The Story of Luke and Marian, Kelsay Books 2019

Keeping in Place, Finishing Line Press 2021

Lira, Poems of a Woodland Woman, Redhawk Publications 2021

Precious the Mule, Redhawk Publications 2022

Contents

Foreword by David A, Shapiro, PhD, CCC, SLP	9

I.

Trouble	15
Hot Summer Sweat	16
Mean Kids and Me	17
Fear in the Fourth Grade	18
Fragile at Fourteen	19
Shame	20
Sudden Stutters	21
Stutter Mysteries	22
Try and Keep Trying	23
Where I Belong	24
High School	25
Call Myself Sister	26

II.

Fear	29
Mentor Myself	30
Never Give Up	31
Turning Strong	32
Career Path	33
Trauma and the Telephone	34
Put Someone on Who Can Talk	35
Grow Respect	36

III.

Starters	39
Under Story	40
Baby	41
Born to Walk	42

Sing	43
Big Changes	44
My Own Child	45
Count on Life	46
Turtle Talk	47
Silk Patches	48
Totem	49

IV.

Stutter into Spring	53
Tribute and Hope	54
Manifesto	55
Stutters and Changes	56
Go to the Wild	57
Speak Easy	58
After	59
When I Still Dreamed of Being Normal	60
Walnut	61
Teach at Last	62
Beyond Stutters	63

V.

Phoenix Rising	67
I Hear the River Call My Name	68
Getting Along Now	69
Fires Creek	70
Thank You, Long Years Later	71
Wonder	72
Like an Extrovert in the Rain	73
Legacy	74
Uneven Rains	75
Acknowledgments	76
Bio	77

Stutters

Stutters: A Book of Hope
Foreword

Mary Ricketson describes herself as a Certified Mental Health Counselor and a Blueberry Farmer. Over the 35 years I have known Mary, first within a professional context and since as friends, I have learned that Mary is much more. She is a devoted mother and family member; she is a woman committed to social justice; she is a community leader, mentor, and teacher; she is an axis of positive change. And she is a person who stutters.

Mary's preceding seven books of poetry are unique in that they are personal reflections of her own life and world and, particularly, the healing power and wonderousness of nature. This book, *Stutters: A Book of Hope*, is particularly personal. It focuses on an intimate, lifelong companion and how Mary's relationship with that companion both evolved over time and influenced every aspect of Mary's life. That daily companion is stuttering.

For readers who might be unaware, stuttering is a universal disorder of speech fluency. In the United States alone, there are over three million people who stutter. In the world, there are over 70 million. Stuttering interferes with the most human element of all – being able to tell one's story by using the words one wants when one wants; "I do," "I love you," "I'm sorry." Rather, speech often is produced with audible or silent blocking, repetitions, prolongations, interjections, broken words, circumlocutions (i.e., saying a word other than the one intended), excess tension, and more. If speech and language uniquely distinguish us as human, being unable to share one's thoughts can render that person feeling other than or, most often, less than human.

James Earl Jones, an American stage and television actor, has a distinctive baritone voice, used as the voice of Darth Vader in *Star Wars* and Mufasa in the original production of *The Lion King*. As a person who stutters, Jones shared the significance of stuttering by saying, "One of the hardest things in life is having words in your heart that you can't utter." I too am a person who stutters. For nearly my first 20 years, stuttering consumed me. My dog, Buddy, was the only living thing to which I could communicate. Oddly, people who stutter can speak fluently with a pet or when alone, just as they can sing without stuttering. I swore an oath to Buddy that if I could find a way to talk, I would do my best to help others find their voice. By providing clinical service, teaching, and conducting research for nearly 50 years, I have honored that promise with people who stutter, their families, and professionals around the world.

Stuttering has been described as an iceberg. What is seen above the surface are the observable symptoms. Most of stuttering, however, the related thoughts and feelings, often reside hidden, below the surface. In this book, Mary shares with the world the entire iceberg that is her stuttering. As a child, Mary viewed her stuttering as a *force of nature*, a force so strong that made her feel powerless. That vulnerability influenced her life in myriad ways. Over time and with the benefit of life experience, maturity, and earned wisdom, Mary has come to view stuttering as *a part of nature*.

Mary initially shared her inner child's experience of embarrassment and shame, confessing "I don't see the sunshine, don't hear birds sing." "I'm a tree with broken limbs, bark broken from my trunk." Yet, all the while, she retained youth and hope, conveying "I believe in a magical world." Later and older, Mary likens herself to an oak tree - strong, withstanding storms, still youthful and embracing hope. She writes, "Hope becomes a sound to believe." Here she proclaims her self-acceptance, "Redbirds sing soft, fly the air as if we've always been safe, here in our own skin."

So, this book is part reflection, part treatise with oneself and the universe, and part memoir. Mary welcomes us into her world and invites us to walk with her along the chronology of her life. While stuttering is universal, there is nothing as unique as one's own voice. Here we experience the evolution of Mary's voice, from faltering and timid as a child, to one of courage, confidence, and conviction. Mary's poems are a medium so perfectly befitting her profound message – Hope is everlasting; positive change is ageless; authenticity and love are precious and irreplaceable.

Stutters

Mary teaches us that stuttering, or any other personal challenge, need not define us. Never the victim, only we can define ourselves. Through much of Mary's life, her stutter is a thing to be confronted, a seemingly insurmountable noun. Remarkably, Mary's stutter becomes a verb - an action, a force, a calling to nature that beckons. "Step quick, straddle sticks, stones, clumps of rich soil stutter into beauty." "Go if rainfall stutters to an end." "Stutter short rows of garden, plant food where rich bottom land sits beside the stream."

In other words, Mary's relationship with stuttering moves from one of separateness and detachment, where stuttering is an object to be controlled if not silenced, to one of unity, mutuality, presentness, and reciprocity, where stuttering is essential to an intimate and long-term partnership. Martin Buber (Austrian and Israeli philosopher, 1878-1965) might have described this relationship as moving from "I, It" to "I, Thou." I believe Mary would confess that her life and actualization as a person were influenced positively more *because* of her stuttering than *in spite of* her stuttering. In closing –

To readers – As you prepare to walk with Mary on her life's path, remember to put on some good hiking boots; you'll be on some rough terrain. Wear a hat and sunglasses; you'll experience patches of bright sunlight. Bring all your senses; you will be surrounded by wildlife, serenaded by mountain streams, and immersed in diverse flora and fauna.

To Mary – Thank you for sharing yourself, for reminding others, through your example, always to be hopeful, loving, real. Beauty exists; the challenge is to remain strong, committed, and able to experience it. Nature is Our North Star.

David A. Shapiro, Ph.D.
Robert Lee Madison Distinguished Professor Emeritus
Speech-Language Pathologist (CCC-SLP, BCS-F)
Western Carolina University
Communication Sciences and Disorders
Cullowhee, North Carolina
June 2023

I.

Stutters

Trouble

I'm eight years old. Other people talk for me.

I try to green and grow like this field, natural.
Hope says I'll spring up when sunshine and weather
say it's time. Neighbor fields grow on their own.
Why not me?

I want my words to pop-out pretty like daffodils,
full of grace, unique petals and colors. If only
my words could be a work of art in a big bunch
like these flowers. If words could flow in rhythm,
one after another.

My words get stuck. Mouth moves good, then contorts.
First no sound, just jammed inside, then the dreaded
sounds repeat. Over and over not a word, but the horrible
sound, then long grotesque noises, more mouth spasms.
Next an arm or foot joins in attempt to say, *Hello*,
or answer, *Mary*, to *What's your name, little girl?*

I let people talk for me. My family is embarrassed.
Teachers want to get on with the class. I lose the spelling
bee even when I know every word. Sometimes I can
whisper an arithmetic answer to a classmate. She raises
her hand, gets the credit. We become friends. I make sure
I get A's on written work.

I make a magical world. I believe in miracles.

Hot Summer Sweat

In some Southern way, we didn't talk about my stutters,
not like we talked about easter egg hunts, plans for new
dresses, or who's expecting another baby. Hot summer
sweat clogged the pores of our words.

Spanish moss hung low from live oak limbs, draped
the discomfort. Embarrassed most of the time,
not many other feelings came my way.

I thought my stutters would stand up and walk off
unnoticed. One day I'd feel alive among people,
same as when I walked alone on damp sand, Gulf
surf washing my feet clean while the tide rolled in.

Stutters

Mean Kids and Me

Children tease, mock, mimic,
not like the mockingbird in the tree,
not sweet repeats of redbirds
and chickadees in flight.

Kids my age copy my dreaded stutter,
exaggerate sounds I hate, get in my face.
I can't erase my fear from myself.

I'm ten now. My talk is all stumble,
falter, and stammer. Mean stuff keeps
me scared, keeps me apart. I try and try
to disappear, nowhere to hide.

On the playground it's fun, just play
and laugh, no talk, go with the flow.

Sometimes I'm one of the crowd.
I join in when we walk past Cathy's
house, make a face, hold our breath
and cross our fingers so we don't get
her "cooties," then we all giggle.
Later guilt festers, keeps me awake
at night. I don't want to be a mean kid.

I pray and promise to find my way.
Learn from this oregano that grows
even between patches of weeds.
Kale comes on when it's cold.
Good stuff happens, even with the bad.

Mary Ricketson

Fear in the Fourth Grade

Essential read aloud time winds me up, a coil
stuck in my throat, tangles of fear, no way to unravel.

Teacher calls on students at random. Know the place,
prove you pay attention. Hear your name. Stand up.
Read till teacher says, *Thank you*.

Constant worry, keep pace with one finger, speed ahead,
rehearse words, imagine sounds, hope to speak easy.

Next name is mine, she says *Mary*. Quickly stand up.
My new plan- get up fast, before I get scared, before panic
turns and turmoils into stutter.

I start. I can do this. Words smooth, I'm doing this good.
But no. Big interruption six-words in. All thirty pairs
of eyes stare at me. Something stupid happened.

She said, *Barry*, not *Mary*. I sit. Tall Barry stands slow,
starts to read. Easy, no concern, no worry in the world.

Quickly I shrink, dig a hole under my desk, crawl in.

Stutters

Fragile at Fourteen

Strangers talk to me at the bus stop, detect my stutter.
Full of grown-up authority, each dispenses sudden
unrequested advice on the spot:

Speak French or Spanish, not your native tongue.
You stutter on your name, so call yourself Ann.
Relax, just relax, relax- on command.
Desperate, I heed every word, fail every time.

My mother's friend visits France, brings back holy
water from Lourdes, place the Virgin Mary appeared
to Bernadette in 1858. Praying for a miracle, Mother
anoints my tongue with this holy water every day.

I don't see the sunshine, don't hear the birds sing.
Vulnerable, I'm a pink rosebud bit back by freeze.
I learn to despise advice, fashion walls around me,
silent defense without solution.

Tension grows like weeds, too many to keep away.
I learn to avoid, speak only when need demands,
hope to shine full bright like stars in the deep of night.

Later and older, I become an oak tree, strong and steady
in rain, snow, and storm. Pileated woodpeckers pound
messages of hope. One bald eagle soars above.

Shame

It was like I spilled deep red spaghetti
on my best white dress,
all down the front
in the middle of people who never knew me,
women and men who by simple human existence
appear important,
definitely privileged to judge me.

I am a spectacle of careless inconsideration,
deplored, lamented, un-forgiven.

I quietly step back, back,
small imperceptible movements.
I fade into invisibility,
oblivion, no words to explain.

Stutters

Sudden Stutters

Cool morning breeze clears the night. Crows caw-caw
when sunshine starts. The rooster across the cove
announces a new day begins.

Family memory says I spoke clear as morning music till
I was seven. Sudden stutters started when I got a real bad
beating from my mother, punishment for hitting a playmate.
No child of mine hits another child!
B-b-b-bu-bu-but, I struggled to say, not a chance to report
that the girl made up rules- *If the ball touches your left cheek,*
you have to hit the cheek of the one who threw it. I did,
and she ran inside the house, told on me.

Hours after punishment, I got to tell my side. I was heard
and believed, but I always stuttered after that, no matter what.
Mystery mixed with sunshine and starlight. Birds called
from the air as always. Life goes on, no matter what.

Mother tried her best to teach us right from wrong and found
new ways to reward and reprimand, but she never spanked
us ever again.

Mary Ricketson

Stutter Mysteries

I jump up and down on the small plank porch. I'm excited,
four years old, on the second story landing of a converted
World War II barracks, home in 1952.

I see the Chevy. Daddy's coming, bringing my big brother
home from kindergarten. Yay! I keep jumping for joy,
then I fall off the edge, ten feet to the ground, hit my head.

Daddy runs from the car, throws the car keys in the air, never
finds them. Mother grabs the other keys, frantic rush down
the stairs. We go to the emergency room, ex-ray, check-up.

They declare me ok, but a long time later, I'm grown up,
stutter for years and years, we all wonder out loud
what the ex-ray might not have shown.

Stutters

Try and Keep Trying

Seasons change like winter to spring and back again.
One man listens, next man makes a face, turns away quick,
a woman interrupts or takes a guess at what I try to say.
I'm ten, thirteen, sixteen.

Wind blows unexpected in this mountain gap. Clouds
cover sun, then warm rays peek-a-boo back and forth.
Talk comes easy sometimes, then turns on me, falls
me down. I'm a tree with broken limbs, bark broken
from my trunk, bruises way down to heartwood.

An exotic adult brings clean pink plastic pebbles,
places them in my mouth. *Practice to talk, mouth
full like Demosthenes, 400 BC. Pebbles fixed
his stammer, might help you too.*
I try.

A normal woman brought me a pencil. *Use any pencil,*
she said, *bite down, pencil in mouth, talk to this microphone
and tape recorder. Distorted sound of your own voice
will change your pattern. You won't stutter if you do it right.*
I try and try.

Next, both parents take me to a hypnotist. I discover
my first b-b-b-but, re-live a violent time, get a post
hypnotic suggestion to re-train my brain not to stutter.
I try my best.

I'm a wildflower in early spring, pop up happy season
to season, bloom full-petal and color, but not always
the same. My sounds change with the sun, wind, rain,
and secrets like mysteries unrevealed.

Mary Ricketson

Where I Belong

Struggle starts from sound to word, push
on to speak my thought, to claim my place,
stutter or not.

In a world where everyone else seems
already to belong, I sound like no one else.
Tension mounts as my sounds repeat.
Life-long ways, fluent or freak, struggle
might always be one sound away.

This small purple crocus pops up in my yard
every year a surprise, same spot or close by,
maybe multiplies its flowers, maybe not.
Might last a week or just a day, take it as it is,
useful for unique beauty, however its display.

I hope my life is like that crocus, one of a kind,
to hear and accept, however I speak and bloom,
purpose and function profound, far from perfection.

Stutters

High School

Gulf breeze blows a strong, sudden change.
Seagulls call one last time. Live oaks go quiet.
We move across country again, mid eighth grade.

Dig into adventure. Learn about snow. Struggle
with galoshes. Desperate to fit in, find new friends,
soften my stutter-fears, find a smile.

Study hard, catch up to new standards. Be good
at schoolwork, excel to outshine my stutters.
Button up my new coat. Snowflakes fall like magic.

Ride a bus to high school. Never miss a school dance.
Move to the music, rhythm speaks well, no need
to talk. Keep time to the tempo, my toes never stutter.

Find my way with new peers, fun in spite of stammers,
jeers, jolts, and urges to cures that never work, then
move back to old friends across country again.

High school will end in two years. Study hard, become
accepted in the honor society like my girlfriends. Get
a good boyfriend, full of adventure. Watch him move away.

Camelias bloom, then magnolias. Think of college. Never
talk of details beyond the clan of family and church. Secret
plans grow. My silent adventure hides from the sun.

Call Myself Sister

Follow the family plan. Leave live oaks, tall pines,
sandy beaches. Move seven hundred miles north.
Enter a convent, age eighteen, expect to live as a nun
all my life, teach school, pray and do good works.

Be like Sister Mary Joseph and Sister Annunciata,
my schoolteachers. Call myself Sister Mary Alice,
follow the call of my vocation, join a holy family.
Live the best life I know.

Wake at five a.m. to pray. Rotate assigned chores,
share a community life. Believe a miracle will end
my stuttering. Go to speech therapy forty miles away,
arranged by Mother Superior.

Stutter and struggle through classes. Study, meditate,
sing, and have fun. Make friends, peers who understand
and don't poke fun. Love this trusted family. Learn
to live in community spirit.

Enjoy long silent times when talk is not allowed.
Attend college classes. Cover my own hair with a veil.
Prepare for vows of poverty, chastity, and obedience.
Hope always for my miracle, to talk with ease and grace.

Overhear a soft conversation of elders who make decisions:
*She does not respond to speech therapy. We can make
her a bookkeeper, so she won't have to talk much.
She cannot teach school like this.*

Shock of my life, I steal away unseen, forever changed.
I can't do numbers, file papers, and be happy. Two plus
two equal four several times in a row, then I add variety.
I'd fail at that job. Living here, I have to obey.

Take two weeks to dwell on this dilemma, watch a hard rain
fall. Find no way to argue against superiors about my life
to come. I can choose now, before the day of solemn vows.

I pack the few things I still call my own, return to my parents,
walk the sandy beach, hear a seagull call, plan my new life.

II.

Stutters

Fear

      walks in,
stares me in the eye
until finally I blink.

Fear gets a toehold.
I hardly know he's here,
so illusive, such a sleuth.

Yesterday he set up camp
while I was unaware.
I thought myself protected,
a guard at every post.

I finished my chores,
sat to rest, to enjoy sunset
and a goodnight kiss.

But fear was in my chair,
on my table, and in my bed,
commanding my attention,
demanding one dance
before I rest.

Now I have no choice.
I know not the tempo
or the time involved.
I submit.

I dance with fear,
my eyes wide open,
looking for his eyes to blink.

Mentor Myself

And the time came when the risk to remain tight in a bud was more painful than the risk it took to blossom.
                                                            Anias Nin

White plumes of foam flower hide among fiddlehead ferns
near an unnamed creek, show themselves when forced
to spike tall, still seen only by one who looks past a show
of purple phlox and native orange flame azalea.

Walk away from that convent, Sisters of Mercy, habits
of blue and white, songs of Alleluia and vows for life.
Stop hiding that summer. Stutter-step to find a world,
speak for myself, no veil to conceal stutters and fear.

One pale breasted chickadee flits about, lands on a wire,
looks me straight in the eye then flies far away. A brown
mule turns her head halfway around, stares agreement
as I walk by.

Move to a new city for college, nineteen years old.
Fear and lonely rise like stone walls and unflowered
hedges. Learn directions, place new faces, find food,
new friends and my own bed.

Mantra myself. Sing silent, *Climb every mountain, ford
every stream.* Sing, *When you walk through a storm,
hold your head up high.* Sing over and over, till it's true.
Walk with rhythms of sounds and melody.

Mentor myself. Pretend to be brave till brave becomes me,
natural as oaks and walnuts leaf out in spring. Stutter along,
always look up. One day a bald eagle soars above, circles
again and again. Now a red-tailed hawk sits on a wire,
anchors the way, day by day.

Stutters

Never Give Up

College classes, campus life, teach me- dodge storms, learn
to never leave myself, never give up.

My sounds, my stutters, defy most traditional techniques.
Finally, the therapist places a metronome on a table.
One sound per beat. Stutters can't happen in rhythms of song.
Practice in the clinic, but, *Don't talk sing-song in public.*
Add inflections, change of pitch.

Hear the pileated woodpecker pound and pound, jackhammer
sound seems like music. Katydids repeat their song, predict
the start of spring, repeat and repeat. Nature and practice
teach rhythm, my voice responds.

Far from perfect but improved, face a world of classes, friends
and public, stay very conscious of how I speak.
Every improvement has its fall. Climb to better, fall again.
But now I'm willing, I climb back up. I face anyone now,
never give up.

Sometimes my repeats sound sweet, like red bird on a wire, or
more like a motor breaking down, sometimes my push, push
is silent, sometimes like a nervous wreck, but finally I believe
I'm worth the wait.

Mary Ricketson

Turning Strong

I'm twenty-one, soon to finish college. My miracle
never comes. Stutters still dominate my speech.

School teacher is long gone from my list of goals,
hard search for a job with no talking turns up nothing.
I need to love my work, have to help the world somehow.

Top notch speech therapy in college helps, does not cure.
Time turns season to season. Be like bloodroot now, ready
to bloom petals pure white, wild in the woods, early spring.

I learn to insist with silent eye contact: *Listen to me,
no interruption now.* Next step, talking to one person
at a time seems easier, leads me to try social work,
find my niche. Even if embarrassed, I connect. I can help.

I cover azalea bushes and the roses, protect against late
freeze tonight, try my best to make life work for flowers,
admire broccoli and lettuce who crave the cold. Study,
learn different ways to thrive, for nature and for me.

Stutters

Career Path

Talk to women in their homes, children too,
even when stutters strut harsh and shout like thunder.
Face the world.

My eyes insist a connection, my words say,
I stutter, we'll make this work.
Smile. Speak of how life flows for each person.
Discover the issues, reasons to help, steps to solve.

Believe. Grow hope. Connect and bond:
I have problems too.

Soft sun streaks the sky, filters through tree limbs,
spreads wide inside near windows where we sit.

Jobs and years, learn to be a willow, sway with the wind.

Insults and cruel words pierce like arrows, sudden sting,
cut to bleed. Learn to bend, breathe, stand again.
Speak again.

Chickadee chirps ring out, repeat, repeat, stutter sounds
like songs.

Will my words to be heard today, every today!
Don't back down, adventure this world. Sprout like iris
in early spring, be the winds of change when words get stuck.
Master skills of waiting, till words come like fountain flows.

Finally, the pileated flies low across the cove, cackles
the sound, calls the day his own way, *C-c-c-c-cackle,
c-c-c-cackle, c-c-cackle.*

Trauma and Telephone

Rainstorms fall often, long and hard, years and years. After
the trauma, seven years old, I never come in from the rain.
Words get stuck, sputter out rough, not smooth.

Too young to know why no one has clear vision to guide me
to grow safe, secure, for words to drift easy from my mouth.

Storms come when the family phone rings. Already trained
polite, *Peavey residence, Mary speaking,* my voice always
came clear before.

Now, my faulty stops and starts of sounds, even no-sound,
evoke blank hesitations or rude blurt outs:
What's going on? Simple hang-ups dominate the unseen
caller, unless Mother grabs the phone. I stop answering.

Outside, bird songs play backyard music. Grass grows.
I swim with ease or walk in water ankle deep, then warm
near fires, ignite to learn, love, create.

Teen years, I seldom phone my girlfriends, and I might miss
dates if boys call. Sounds don't leave my mouth.
Talk in person allows for times of tolerance.

First social work job after college, I stumble words, answer
a desk phone every time. No choice. Struggle on.
Co-workers hear, worry, ask a supervisor how this new
worker will manage the job. Later, I learn he smiled easy,
said, *I think you will find she has a way.*

How have I grown, acorn to oak? Branches broken, twisted,
gnarled and knotted, still hold strong, bear fruit, rise to beauty
of their own. Now those treetop crows speak magic to me,
seem not to care what sound I create.

Stutters

Put Someone on Who Can Talk

Walk in this cold March wind, catch every warm
ray of sun. Watch the mule graze new green grass.
The cow in the field has a new companion.
Everyone needs a friend.

Remember now, early years as social worker,
help abused children to safe arms of protection.
Work long hours and emergencies.

Take a phone call at home after work. Stammer
Hello to the district attorney. Stutter the telling,
legal needs of a small child with breaks and bruises.

Remember the hostile male voice interrupt, *Put someone
on who can talk.* Abrupt, my new boyfriend takes the phone,
You can't talk to her like that! Settled, I finish my report.

Remember now, the new peace, calm, the new respect.

Mary Ricketson

Grow Respect

Move across states, settle where ancient mountains climb
stone to sky. Gain strength from mysteries unknown.

Age twenty-six, help disabled adults. Bridge development,
difficulty, progress. Teach skills in small segments, assist
growth of mind and heart.

Dogwood flowers dot the air. Trilliums bloom their beauty
hardly seen except by those who look beyond grass, weeds,
and poplar saplings in the wild.

Stutters still get in the way, spew storms inside me: stress,
tense tumbles, turns, hard p-push of breath from chest
to tongue. G-get the sounds out, make some sense.
K-keep on till limp, give in to rest.

Frogs croak at night under stars or clouds. Rough repeats,
sounds gruff and guttural, still sing a symphony of pleasure.

Try graduate school after work, love it, do it well, stutters
be damned. Rise above ways to make my words. Begin
a new job, counselor for mental health, deep issues men
and women hold and hide.

Attend community meetings. Find facts of women beaten
and battered. Lead a task force, build resources,
start programs, reach for help.

Hide myself. Count on others to speak in public. Fear
words and sounds. Try to avoid storms of stutters,
always present.

Get the job done. Be embarrassed. Cry alone at night.
Be the helper people seek out for help, day by day.
Grow respect. Talk one to one. Hide from groups if I can.

Mist rises from the frog pond, mends wounds from stutter
sounds, pains of trouble. White wildflowers will open
when sunshine comes out to warm the way.

III.

Stutters

Starters

My dad always moved his mouth a little, just silent
lip-stutters, hardly noticed, a way to get started
before pronouncing perfect sounds of words.

We don't know all the genetics we'd like to know,
and we don't hold out for cures. Live, live every day.

Habit now, learned and practiced in college speech
therapy, I place my tongue-tip to the roof of my mouth
before I speak my first word, a way to get started.

Rhythm starts my talk. Hours, months, years, practice
talking to the beat of a metronome, find a pace. Repeat
well past boredom. Add inflection, break the sing song.

Be like a morning bird, cheery chirp-chirp over and over.
More fluent, less stutter, use what works, always practice.

Under Story

Sweet bird song under cloud cover,
chickadee chirps sound personal
refrains for me on this pensive day.

Red clover among field grass remembers
sunshine, tempts fate, then seems to sleep.
Solomon seal droops delicate petals unseen.

Wild cherry trees swoosh their new leaf
growth and white flower-tendrils in the wind.
A rain crow coos, *Swing on up to sing with me.*

Five deer stand in respect, seem to speak
reverent words in silence. One red and black
pileated woodpecker hides high, cackles a grin.

Tulip poplars populate blossoms, drop
petal clusters of flower, keep uninvolved
in chaos of unspoken words.

Fear feeds tensions, stutters and repeats,
symptoms of neurological origin, jitters
and stammers that pop up like poison ivy.

Interruptions of natural notes of music
and flow cause trouble in the spoken world.

Free to be silent all day, worries and strains
and stutters travel down-creek in peace.

Stutters

Baby

I'm thirty-eight years old, seven months pregnant.

Mountain mint thrives in clumps wild as wind
whistling in this Appalachian cove. Dogwoods
sport first bursts of flower. Morgan horses rest
in a field of green grass and trust.

Today's newspaper column mentions excellent
work of the National Stuttering Project. Look
up details. Attend a regional meeting in Atlanta,
two hours away.

What if my child speaks with stutters, as I do?
What if s-s-s-sttt-op- and p-p-p-p-lease cause
uproar, ridicule and sleepless nights? Fear runs
me into circles. Will I pass the gene, the shame,
fights and struggles of a too-hard life?

Vow to find the way to make life good for my child.
Count on wild woods to inspire, heal scars of forest
fires, bloom pretty mountain laurel and rhododendron
like magic when times are right.

Flow like clear creek water, change with weather,
rocks, and winds. Even the endangered salamander
gains protection.

Born to Walk

In the dark
hallways where ghosts
of ages lurk, my history
hides and waits.

I prepare myself.
No backpack. No tent.
Only water for the washing.

I was born to walk
where angels do not live,
where invisible demons
lie in wait, pretend to love.

Before I die
my journey will cut down
ancient icons of a time
when eyes were closed
and memories were zipped shut.

What else is there to do?
I must hike a trail
too dark for trees,
too narrow for two.

Stutters

Sing

Sing soft, like redbirds and morning chickadees
when light begins a fresh new day. No regret lingers.
We don't stutter when we sing.

Sing out, *Help*, or *Fire*, if you can't spit it out fast.
Words flow fluent in rhythm of song.

Sing happy, sing sad, sing the message to a machine
that won't wait for stutters. Sing calm, sing rage,
and always sing love.

Read Shakespeare in a group. We won't stutter
when we speak in multitudes.

Run words like a river. Stutter natural over rocks,
boulders, blocks. Sound out change in wiggles, ripples
of eddies. Water of surprises, beauty stutters along,

hides speckled trout in deep river holes, protects fish
and treasures by shade from low slung limbs. Stutters
of the river keep secrets, mystery twists of winding flow.

Big Changes

Give birth to a baby boy, widen the world where I live,
welcome new life and delight. Age thirty-eight.
Grow myself into a mother. Wonder if he will stutter.
Promise everything safe, healthy, happy for my child.

Change work roles. Open my own therapy office, alone.
Stutter through h-h-hello to answer the telephone, no one
else here to speak for me. Make it work.

Late freeze brings danger to blueberries in the field.
Hard times come in all kinds of ways. Always find a way.

Age 66, mountains of mint double and double in my garden,
and fireworks of celebration fill the skies.
I fly across country, attend my grown son's PhD graduation.

Whatever suffers the stutters- mountains of tension, breath
stuck in the wrong place, head jerks out of control,
arm pumps and eye blinks add to the mix but can't fix it.
Life rises to the top.

Believe in yourself, I taught my son. Reach for the stars
and beyond.

Stutters

My Own Child

Fear erupts, a volcano asleep until my son stutters.
First words flow fluent- mama, dada and the rest,
but stutters start soon, then a tearful complaint,
Something's stuck.

Shame of my own lies long underground,
but I cannot hide anymore.

Years and years, I don't speak of my stutter, act like
I don't do it, don't hear it. Shine my best self forward,
ignore, ignore.

My best is like bright white petals of blood root flowers,
woodland wild plants that sprout up among winter weeds
in early spring. Later the purple glow of wild geranium
stands tall and proud. Make my way, stand alone,
show my best, ignore the rest.

I grow flowers above my shame, unaware that what hides
below always comes to surface.

Now I re-shape my own tree branches, alter my ways, talk
about stuttering, my own and my son's.

Find an expert. Get the right help. Learn biology, genetics,
basic strategies, new brain discoveries.
Give time for him to grow out of it. He does not.

Re-make myself, fit the need. Speak up for him at school-
no shame, no rush, no interrupt. Help the teachers help
my child. Be a willow, weep with beauty, best when
branches bend with the wind, graceful adapt
to times of change.

Mary Ricketson

Count on Life

Moon, three days off full, shines brilliant in the eastern sky.
Wind blows irregular gusts, swooshes treetops like stutters
and sputters.

Frog calls stammer ribbit-repeats from the pond, low sounds
of grunt-gross, strong with wonder. Crickets hum,
not a stumble. Dark falls fast, cold sets in, strong breeze calls
with its own song.

Morning comes on full bright. Redbirds sing. Field grass
sways a graceful waltz till irregular gusts and spurts of wind
stammer, tamper, tempt a syncopated beat.

Garden chores call while day is new. Push tall stakes
into the soil by each row of peas. Tie three lines of string
to start their climb. Let tendrils stutter, start to hold,
hope they smooth along with age.

Add more cords, stair steps as growth requires. Count on
grey rocks to steady this earth, count on life to reach
whatever good may come.

Stutters

Turtle Talk

When dogwoods finally bloom, dot forest edges with white,
and warm sweeps of spring start, stutter, and stop, we find
the expert, only a two-hour drive from home.

Our child engages, learns to talk like a turtle, not a rabbit.
Slow and easy sounds slide out. No magic, no cure, more
control to make a way for less tension, more smiles.

Long roads along a rushing whitewater river inspire rhythms
and resilience of life. We travel this way for help, steady on,

make ourselves good models of slow, turtle speech at home,
consult often at school, request the teacher who talks slow,
and link with local help to bridge new skills.

Harsh winds still blow, and storms have their way. Seasons
change and change again. Hope becomes a sound to believe.

Silk Patches

Pain of old sits on attic shelves
or buried leagues under,
still festers wide open
when wind blows hot and dry.

Clean cut this time,
fresh wounds from the past,
blood red

pain feels new,
slices layers of scars
healed over by time,
desperate need, a will to live.

Turn around quick,
before paralysis sets in
again, before death gets a grip.

Find your old silk coat,
patches sewn on well,
still a perfect fit.
Wear it well,
walk straight into the sun.

Stutters

Totem

A lion came to me today,
brought me to my power,
the splendor and magic that is mine.
With frenzied mane his face
changed into the little girl from the woods,
the one I early learned to shun from me,
the one Mother never would allow
to come out in me to play.

All grown up and welcome now,
I am to roar into the face of danger.
I am to hunt in cooperation with the rest,
and only hunt for what I need.
I am wild as the wind.
I harm no one who does not harm me.
I steal away from danger if I can.
I know my rightful place.

I am protector of the child within.
I play and laugh and seek adventure.
I do not do every task in life.
There are other energies for that.
Friends and family in my pride
join hands with me in rich support.
I was made for teaching,
joining with others for healing.

It comes from a red arrow
that pierced me young.

IV.

Stutters

Stutter into Spring

When redbuds bloom soft purple along Joe Brown Highway
and forsythia sports wild spires of yellow bells, days grow
longer. Cold comes back and forth so much that sunshine
can't overcome. Temperature stutters itself d-down, down
below freezing. Blueberries live on, burst through obstacles,
make their fruit, fulfill the cycle, escape the freeze this time,
stutter through natural obstacles.

Early morning sounds of pittttt, pitttt, pitttt pound the pine
tree-trunk loud, heard all over this mountain cove. Next,
crisp sounds of c-cackle, c-cackle, c-cackle blurt, repeat
as the black and red beauty glides the sky, settles easy,
out of sight deep in the woods to rest.

Mary Ricketson

Tribute and Hope

For Nancy Simpson

C-c-can I be in your writing c-class? My shy
voice on the phone. Late summer sun sinks
slow in the west. Seconds seem like hours.
Of course, you can be in my class…

Over and over, years and years, attend a weekly
class, fall in love with words, sounds, rhythms,
creations, learn to follow a path of poetry, listen
to writers more skilled than me and less, take
my turn, read my own words to other learners.

Grow with the walnut tree down field, seasons
leaf, nut, bare-limb, bark more rugged every year.

Age fifty, other people listen to words I create
into verse. Students side by side listen. I stutter
my words on and on. Word creations win over
struggle, red face of embarrass, fears, sounds
always hard to push out into words.

Mountain laurel blooms pink, covers creek banks
and hillsides like quilt pieces, warms the air
with promise, ease, and hope.

*Now you must read your poems at the public
monthly program. Prepare to read twenty
minutes of your original work.*

I can't. Exempt me, I plead. Nancy teaches
special ed by day, pushes me past my limits:
You write, you have to read, it's what poets do.
I obey, suffer, stutter, and struggle. People listen.
People applaud. I keep on. Crafted words, sounds,
and images carry me.

Years later, as redbirds land on dogwood blossoms,
I speak on stage at Nancy's memorial.

Stutters

Manifesto

My body knew
before my mind
made thoughts,
before my voice
found words.

Make peace with loss.
Make friends with change.

A candle flickers.
Blue light drowns
in its own flame.
Secret shards
of hope surrender.

Let me live
where crystal clear creeks
slither over small stones,
ripple over rugged rocks,
slide through the smooth,
and rain and tears are welcome
as sunlight and laughter.

Where birth and death
run the same river bed,
I run my life.

Stutters and Changes

A storm warning starts the day, hours before daylight,
then finally clears after I sit an hour, safe under the stairs.

Walk the new day when calm returns. Pink blossoms fill
the gravel road, petals blown off the weeping cherry tree.

Neighbor Jill's dog stands like a statue, seems on watch,
looks like a wolf, warns me of some looming change.

Mist rises. Drops fall, not quite rain, sky comes slow
to clear. Quiet world, only birdsong and my footsteps exist.

Memories and turmoil of my past return:

I'm young, stutters torture me like storms all the time.
I learn to drive the family sedan, grow up, get my own car,

struggle to say **Fill 'er up***, like my dad, and,* **Check the oil**
please*. Years pass. At last I feel the rhythms of my voice,*

sense how sounds can slide, small enough stutters
not to shock, not to make eyes pop with questions like,

What's wrong with you?

Finally, I speak well enough, not so scared of filling stations,
but suddenly the whole world changes to self-serve gas.

Stutters

Go to the Wild

Wind and woods call in every weather,
play Wildwood Flower on limbs of trees,
entice like sounds of ancient selkie songs.

Run the rutted dirt path into the wilds
today, tomorrow, forever, falter on.

Go to the woods where stutters soften
song. Step quick, straddle sticks, stones,
clumps of rich soil stutter into beauty.

Go when morning sun dapples down
the pines, syncopated irregular rays.

Go if rainfall stutters to an end, washes
rocks clean and sprouts fern fronds,
sputter through puddles and all.

Go when flowers first bloom, stay to see
petals fall down to the forest floor.

Step into the wild where wise wanders
on the breeze and life wills itself to go,
to keep life every season.

Speak Easy

Fifty-five years old now, I'm in the driver's seat, my dad
the passenger. Dogwoods and wildflowers bloom along
country roads, sharp mountain curves, then cultured flowers
flourish the sides of Interstate 40. We drive almost the whole
length of North Carolina, to East Carolina University.

Dad keeps me steady on this trip, hopes to help resolve
what he could not solve when I was a little girl.

We seek a new invention, the *Speech Easy*, a hearing aid case
equipped with metronome sound and slight delayed feedback,
two techniques to ease my speech, flow my words well-
if it works.

Meet staff, inventor, and facilitator. Take a test. Practice
with a sample device. Read aloud. Talk casual, proceed
to harder situations. Step by step, respond to training, receive
instructions for use on my own, as close to cure
as I have ever come, words finally fluent more than stutter.

Our drive home, full of hope, sparks questions.
Will this device and my response hold up to real life, day
by day, all the ways of words and obstacles? Will fear
of talking still stress and dominate my time?

Home arrives. Real life is where I left it. Device hidden
behind my ear, I talk. People I know ask me what happened,
where did my stutters go? I break a harsh cycle
long practiced, talk smooth now, partner with peace.

I still stutter into small obstacles, less often than before.
Confidence claims my new road.

Stutters

After

Quiet, after stammers,
clamors and hullabaloo,
fear crawls back to a cubby
hole, embarrassed now
to have sounded alarm.

Solomon seal starts to bloom
beside a one lane road. White
dogwood flowers gleam full
in sunshine, pure and spotless.

Redbirds sing soft, fly the air
as if we've always been safe,
here in our own skin.

Mary Ricketson

When I Still Dreamed of Being Normal

I shut my mouth, ashamed, afraid
to speak in stutters, draw silent shuns
and loud ridiculous shocks of disbelief,

got good at quiet ways, learned
to like solo, silent, speechless times,
created ideals in my mind:

Pretend to be mute. Hope to be called
to the blackboard, never stand and recite.
Grow flowers. Sew seams. Clean, cook
and serve. Babysit, dance, hike.

Later, dreams aside:
Un-learn the word *can't*.
Push myself to talk.
Believe my own words.
Never give up.

Stutters

Walnut

Suddenly I remember
life is hard.

One walnut tree stands
at the end of my field.
Forty years I watch. It never wanders
never moves, only sheds its leaves,
drops its weakest branches
when storms rage through the cove.

What is a woman,
but a tree that walks around?
Storms and seasons leave scars
on ripened beauty,
carve hearts in the bark
where mysteries of strength lie
in the eyes of each beholder.

No decision diverts the tree.
A tree does not worry about its fate.
Straight and tall
it stands
through all seasons.

Teach at Last

I'm sixty-five years old, a therapist thirty-five years.
Will you teach psychology at the college part time?
Surprise request, time of change, fear steps aside.
I say yes, make space between scheduled office clients.

Apply, get vetted and approved. Teach the science
and art of helping. Re-visit my dream, my wish
for a miracle, to talk with words fluent enough to teach.
Plan lessons, plan class time, plan how to talk. Believe.

Drive to campus twice a week, meet students nineteen
years old to fifty. Cold winds and snow of January
break to new green grass of spring fever, early pastel
blooms. Students make plans for new lives and careers.

If stutters stop me, please keep eye contact, listen.
Don't finish for me. We will get through this together.

Introduce myself, speak of my stutter, avoid shock. Allay
fears and embarrassment. Stutters come few, short, less
tense than before. Still I fear stares, remarks that blurt,
pierce, embarrass. Fear the past, fear the unknown.

Wind outside rustles poplar trees outside, *w-w-whir,*
w-w-whir, w-w-o-o-sh, k-k-krack, and swirl to quiet.

Students laugh about my crazy socks, ask questions,
practice new skills, confide two by two. I tell them
it was my dream, long ago, to be a teacher. We breathe
a group sigh of relief for dreams come true.

When I speak fluent, *s-s-s-stutters* interrupt, but never
shut down class. No crass remarks, no one leaves.

Accept some stutters. Forget the miracle that never came.
I can talk now. I can make myself understood. I can teach.
Redbirds sing through classroom windows, cherry trees
spring into flower, dogwoods swell with buds of promise.

Stutters

Beyond Stutters

Stack sticks and twigs, mud pies and stones,
heap piles of rocks and waste. Keep close
by a forest of trees, field of grass and flower.

Tame streams near broad rushing creeks.
Get to know a river with moods of change,
dark to light, serene, pensive, wise, ready
to speak prophesy, then sputter-change, rage
with wild wind and rain.

Stutter short rows of garden, plant for food
where rich bottom land sits beside the stream.
Admire first sprouts, then broccoli, lettuce
and tomatoes. Taste results, preserve, keep on.
Dig deep, determine how life works.

Walk the long lane every afternoon, careful look
for beauty. Purple morning glory stammers-up
corn stalks, threatens kernels before time to harvest.

Make friends with tulip poplar, old and young. See
brambles of life turn to bloom like blackberries,
blossom to fruit. Watch birds fly and wonder how.

Learn this land. Live beyond first glance and chance,
walk off trail. Sit in a small ravine between trees
before full leaf fills the forest floor.

Listen to whistles and calls of birds. Watch out
for snakes, avoid poison ivy. Climb a tree
if you can. Learn the magic of ferns.

Beyond stutters, life blooms deep in the woods.
Find trailing arbutus, wild geranium, bloodroot,
foam flower, trillium, and lady slipper.

In late light before dusk, spy a lone jack-in-the-pulpit
among short weeds at the edge of the woods, waiting
to be seen.

V.

Stutters

Phoenix Rising

Slow raindrops almost stop. Walk in the wet
before full drench returns. Rain decides the day.

Take to the easy chair inside, reflect under cabin
roof comfort. Time travel familiar rains of life,

like fungus in the blueberry field, worms invading
corn when it silks, stutters when words need to speak.

Feel the freeze, the stop, question the way forward,
then break away from old vines that return as weeds.

A black crow sits alone on a fence post, caw-calls
the morning breeze like prophesy from the wise

one unseen, but always present. Wait for sprouts
of hope. Watch sunflowers rise after rain.

Mary Ricketson

I Hear the River Call my Name

Hiawassee River winds
where I go to rest my mind
from a hard day of work.
I make my way down to the river.
I walk along grassy banks.

I gaze at ripples.
Granite boulders grip my mind.
I marvel at their strength.
Branches, leaves, and bits
of trash float downstream.

A steady current gentles
through my mind.
A rush of water splashes
up against an edge of rich black dirt
and runs crystal clear.

Dark ripples tear
through the middle.
My raucous thoughts hide
like wild trout hide in the deep.

I slow my pace.
Sounds of running water
rhythm through my thoughts.
I hear the river call my name
and I know what to do.
One by one, I cast my burdens
and watch them float downstream.

Stutters

Getting Along Now

Never would have picked a dog this size, this bark,
but he picked me,

came around, liked my porch, my petting hand,
loved my older hound till her last breath.

Now we get along just fine. I've adapted to this dog's
ways, his size, his bark. He's trained me to it all.

Never would have picked my stutters either. Now
we've made peace together, found our own way
to get along.

Mary Ricketson

Fires Creek

Bluets, Solomon's plume, and laurel
not yet ready for bloom lead the way

along a path next to the rushing waters
of Fires Creek.

Yellow root grows free, multiplies
year by year among the rocks.

Hellbender salamander swims protected.
Native trout hide in the deep.

Leatherwood Falls cascades long, loud
and wonderful after the rain.

Listen well, speak not a word. Morning
mist cleared hours ago, rose to the sky.

Fast waters smooth hard rock edges, smooth
out stutters of words not yet spoken.

Wind carries every care away, and words
will find a way of their own.

Stutters

Thank You, Long Years Later

A summer work student, 18 years old, ready
for college, worked three months in my program
for people with severe mental illness, 1980.

Forty-three years later, she finds me on Facebook:
*You were my boss. I stuttered too. When I saw
you, all you were doing, I knew I could make
a life for myself too.*

Wonder

That black snake already claims his place
in the sunshine, lies there like he belongs
on the walkway out front.

Soon orange daylilies will bloom the hours
of summer. Walnuts already flaunt new leaves,
and the beech tree stands fully caped in green,
shades the ground below.

Kindness and comfort grow on their own.
Sit awhile, life is slow. Marvel at stalks
of tiny star petals called blue-eyed grass.
Watch red clover grow.

Search for pink lady slipper in the woods.
Weave a smooth tapestry of words and nature,
bumps and bruises show up as beauty features.

Stutters

Like an Extrovert in the Rain

Raindrops lay low on soft green poplar leaves, sparkle
in the morning light. Walk now in leftover rain.
Sun wants to shine, wants to initiate strong streaks
and glow, but steady sprinkles go on and on, take the day,
keep it for their own.

Watch cottontails run top speed, stutter-jump across open
coves, get back under woodland cover. See squirrels hop
tree to tree, splatter leaf holds of built-up rain. Step away
if I can.

Circle around puddles in the path. My own footsteps
crunch-crunch on mud and gravel. I'm the first to walk
this path after the rain.

*Always scared when I wait my turn to tell my name, fear
the shock or laughter when I M-M--M-a-ry my name, or seem
dumb if no sound comes out my mouth. Stand up first if I can,
get it out, get it over.*

All the tiny violets appear bright in the damp, like gemstones
scattered around in the grass by secret fairy friends
from the woods. Common daisy fleabane flowers look fresh,
treasures of ages in this rain.

*Learn to speak up first if I can. Phone people first,
suggest first, ask first, gain some slight control when I speak,
avoid the wait, the worry. Shorten the fear, find the rhythm
to ease out the sounds of words. Pretend I like to talk,
until I do.*

Star flowers stay tight, closed like night till bright light opens
like a secret spell. Wild azalea flames orange petals,
fires the day under sunshine beams.

Mary Ricketson

Legacy
Gift from my son on my 75th birthday

Birds sing all morning in this valley, sweet
sound, easy music, not a stutter in the air.

My son, now grown, says to me,
Just that you existed, Mom,
you stuttered, still worked a job
that made you to talk all the time,
made a difference to me.
You had a life, even with stutters,
so I always knew I could too.

Look at this walnut tree today, take
time to notice beyond first glimpse.
Feel the rough, sturdy bark outside,
consider its rich grain of beauty inside.

Dig this dark soil, smooth out clumps
till soft brown granules slip between
open fingers. Plant broccoli, kale, lettuce,
early crops to feed body and hope.

Look at us now, still stutters on the outside,
rich grain, good crop, easy flow inside.

Stutters

Uneven Rains

Rainfall in this forest reveals life apart
from time and traffic. Here, a canopy
of trees breaks flow, sifts the drenching,
sprinkles fall down the forest floor.

Ferns and crawling pine keep damp
for life. Little rocks shine clean.
Fluent raindrops drizzle-up change,
occasional stutter-stairs fall and dump
clumps, plop into splatter like stutter-talk,
splay the world in two, but

deer, squirrels and rabbits do not mind
the sounds of stutter in this forest,
and neither do I.

Soon the air clears, a cool breeze re-sets
the day. Puddled leaves perk up pretty.
Veils of water lift, prepare me for a world
beyond this forest.

Make my talk worth the listen,
my sounds worth the patience,
and let my love of life ring past
falters, stutters, and uneven rains.

Acknowledgements

Old Mountain Press, Down by the Sea Anthology, Hot Summer Sweat

I Hear the River Call My Name, Fear, Manifesto, I Hear the River Call My Name

Hanging Dog Creek, Born to Walk, Walnut

Shade and Shelter, Silk Patches

Mississippi, the Story of Luke and Marian, Totem

Lake Chatuge Living, Getting Along Now, Fires Creek

Your Daily Poem, Wonder

Special thanks to The National Stuttering Association, (formerly National Stuttering Project), John Albach, Naomi King, and to David Shapiro SLP, for helping both me and my son to live well as people who happen to stutter, and to Emory Prescott SLP, Shelby Stephenson PhD, and Diana Smith for inspiration to keep writing Stutters.

For the reader
My stutters began when I was seven years old. For nearly seventy years, stuttering has been, and still is, a daily part of my life. This collection includes aspects of my life that shifted or even developed because I stuttered. I hope you find strength in these poems. Even through struggle, hope rises.
Mary Ricketson

Stutters

Bio

Mary Ricketson's published collections are *I Hear the River Call My Name, Hanging Dog Creek, Shade and Shelter, Mississippi: The Story of Luke and Marian, Keeping in Place, and Lira, Poems of a Woodland Woman, and Precious the Mule*. She won first place in the 2011 Joyce Kilmer Memorial Forest 75th anniversary national poetry contest. Mary's poems reflect the healing powers of nature, path she follows from Appalachian tradition, surrounding mountains as midwife for her words. She is a mental health therapist in private practice in Murphy NC and likes her writing groups, hiking mountain trails, and her garden of vegetables, flowers, and blueberries.

www.ingramcontent.com/pod-product-compliance
Lightning Source LLC
Chambersburg PA
CBHW051704090426
42736CB00013B/2536